WOMEN ARE AMAZING

By

Armando Guerra

WOMEN ARE AMAZING
by Armando Guerra

Table Of Contents

Preface

I would like to thank all those who have encouraged me to write this book — especially my lovely wife of 35 years. Jackie is the true inspiration and main reason I wrote this book. Her unconditional love and support, despite my many shortcomings, helped me to see women as amazing creatures worthy of admiration by those who love them.

Introduction

With so many books on marriage and family life, not to mention lots of TV doctors who give advice on practically everything, why would I decide to write a book on marriage and family life? It's not like I have any degrees hanging on my walls or abbreviated letters after my name.

The fact is that I have always wondered how a Plain Joe, who I believe includes most of us men, sees relationships and how he would realistically explain them from a man's point of view.

It has been said that "the great ambition of women is to inspire love" and how true that is of most women. They are truly the aviators in most relationships. They are the anchors during rough times in this vast sea of humanity in which we live. They are the one piece of the puzzle that makes it all come together to make a wonderful family unit.

Yet, life has taught me that women are under appreciated. They are not given the love and respect they deserve. All women should be cherished when their love is unconditional. Women as a whole don't ask for much in return only that we occasional acknowledge our love for them — a kind word, a tender touch such as a hug or kiss. If you are not the affectionate type, get them a card, beautiful flowers, or on occasion some bling. As a word of advice, the latter two can get you out of the dog house, if you know what I mean. Really gentlemen, do I need to say more.

Unfortunately, I believe that men can't figure this out until we get somewhat older. Perhaps, it's that little boy in us that is at fault. So we act like jerks in the early stages of our relationships, causing unnecessary heartaches to those we love through unkind words, thoughtless remarks, and just plain stupid actions.

This I feel is one of the main reasons for so many divorces throughout the world — a man not following godly principles with regard to how a woman should be treated.

The failure is to acknowledge that a woman is the weaker vessel, not in an inferior way but simply because she is an emotional creature with a makeup that is unique. This requires understanding, if we want to succeed in any relationship. Every woman is different. Yet, they all have one thing in common: they all need love to blossom and deserve our admiration so they can feel good about themselves.

For various reasons women are hard on themselves. At times, they go through stages in life of low self-esteem so it's vital that we always make them feel wanted and loved.

Let me just add, no man should ever abuse a woman physically. That's a man who is a coward. But, we should also be conscience of verbal abuse. This too is not a mark of a true man.

My book at times may take the spin that I am a male chauvinist pig but in reality I am culturally balanced. Remember, the inspiration for this book is the admiration I have for my wife and mother of my two children. I have found the proverbial wife spoken of in the Book of Proverbs' Chapter 31.

CHAPTER 1
Nurtured

The moment we came into this world, we began our lives of being nurtured by a woman, this being our loving mother. We are the apple of their eyes, their little boys. So, in reality, one of the primary reasons for us men being the way we are is that we realistically have been nurtured by a woman most of our lives. Now I am not saying that this is an excuse for our behavior but perhaps an explanation. Let me elaborate.

Our mothers began this journey the moment we began to be breast fed. In my case, I was unique. I was breast fed by two women — doubling my problem. Let me explain. Mom began to breast feed me and then she took ill. Her milk dried up so my aunt, who also had given birth to my cousin relatively at same period of time, breast fed me until my mother got well. So can you blame me for being so spoiled? As we grow up, they continue to spoil us. They wash our cloths, clean our rooms, and prepare our favorite meals. Some of you men know what I am talking about. For some of us in certain cultures this process never ends, even after we get married.

This of course drives your mates up the wall, which is another chapter in itself and one I will address later in the book.

Now, getting back to this theory I have of where our overnurturing problems begin.

After growing up being nurtured practically for a large part of our lives by our mothers, the time comes when yet another woman comes into our lives — our wives or significant other. So, you see, we go from one woman to another, with more feeding of this nurturing mentality for most of our lives.

As we all know, most young wives want to impress their new husbands and, of course, be the new lady in his life. So, the nurturing process begins again. And here we go again!

Let me finish telling you my story as it will give you a better understanding of my theory.

I grew up in a male dominated home of Latin decent. My father did not allow us to do much around his house. My mom and two sisters did most of the chores around the house. While my brother and I watched sports with our dad after dinner. We had lots of sports growing up in New York. Blame it on cable TV if you want.

Dinner was unique, yet in step with our tradition, as I learned while visiting Ecuador, my country of origin. There, in most cases, the men sit at the table and are served their meal. The women do all the work. Interestingly enough, they seem to enjoy performing their duties as a wife and/or mother. To others it's hard to explain but the fact is that they derive a great deal of happiness and joy as they take care of their family duties to those they love.

But if you really think about it, this aspect of life goes way back throughout many families and cultures. If you don't believe me, pickup an old movie or watch *"Little House on the Prairie"* episodes and you will see traditional families practicing this in their households. So, don't be a doubter, keep reading and enjoy my book.

This is how I grew up and to this day, I continue to be a prince at my mom's house. When I first got married, it drove my wife crazy because she just thought I was a spoiled brat, when in reality I was just following my culture and making my mom happy.

Now, why is this story important?

I believe it's a clue as to the reason we begin to have marriage struggles with our mates, especially if we marry away from our traditions or cultures — not in every case but to a large extent.

To this day, I continue to be the prince in my mom's house

It all goes back to the first day you were nurtured by your mother.

After you were weaned, your mom continued to serve your meals, bathe you, and dress you up, and even comb your hair. Think about it — my wife still buys what I wear — my suits, shirts, ties that match, so in reality, she is dressing me up. This makes a lot of sense, as I said.

It continues. As a child, I went to a private school and mom would always make sure I was nice and clean and my uniform ironed. She would always comb my hair. She would say to me: "Someday, I am not going to be able to comb your hair." I asked why. "Because you will be too tall to reach." Those words came true. My mom is about 5 feet tall and I grew to be 5 feet 9 inches tall.

I had a beautifully loving mother. Mom would say farewell everyday when I went to school even through high school. She would get up early every morning to iron my shirts and made sure I had everything I needed for my day.

Yet, despite all this, I still grew up like most young men in those early teen years battling with my mom. I never was completely disrespectful but I talked back, argued, disagreed. Yet, at the same time, I obeyed my mother. No matter how bad I was, she was always there for me, like most moms. Women are amazing creatures. Their love is genuine, real, never ending, no matter what happens. We all go through this phase in our young lives. Believe it or not, it's how we learn to bond with our mothers.

We eventually grow up to appreciate our moms and ultimately make that famous call to mom to let her know how we feel about her.

Have you ever notice that in every sports event where you see the athlete make a home run, a touchdown, a basket? When cameras are on him, he always says "I love you, mom," or "this is for you, mom." Rarely does an athlete say something about his dad. Why? Because he has gotten to appreciate how valuable his mom was in his life. His success to a large degree is due to his mother's loving discipline and support. Our mothers never give up on us. Their love is unique in this respect. Besides, a dad was always busy making a living or out with his friends.

What's most fascinating is I saw all over again this process occurring with my son. His mom dressing him, bathing him, combing his hair, just like my mom combed mine, and, of course, making his lunch. What was most fascinating to me was seeing my son and his mother have constant debates about everything. It seemed like they would argue about something or another practically every day and it all started the moment he became a teenager.

I realized now this combative process is what most young men go through with their moms. This I call the bonding process.

They even playfight a lot during this stage in their young lives. Let me add here that this gives them mix signals because they don't know when to stop. Remember, they are teenagers growing up. Eventually, they learn to pickup their mom's signals, her facial expressions, and tone of voice. This again is the nurturing process I talk about in this book.

Unfortunately, it doesn't stop there. I wish it did because if it did, we would not have so many divorces in the world.

The reality is that for some unknown psychological reason, we revert back to this process with the next woman in our lives. Some have written books about this phenomenon, saying men are from Mars and women are from Venus. Ring a bell? This is how others try to understand or explain why we have problems with our mates.

> **This is how others try to understand or explain why we have problems with our mates.**

My theory is that this is how we bond with the person we love.

We go back to all we know in a relationship. It's not an excuse for our behavior but it makes sense from a physiological point of view. No, I am not a doctor. Yet, think about it. With so many books on the subject and so many experts on this matter, we still can't get it right. Why? Because it's a process we all go through just like we did with our moms. The main difference is that mom never gave up.

Now, don't misunderstand me. I am not making an excuse for acting like a jerk in the beginning of a relationship with a mate, and I am not saying women should understand this process without trying to help us in anyway.

What I know from experience is that eventually we men all grow up between age 34 and up, and we begin to appreciate our mates and to show them the love and respect they deserve. We need only to remember our marriage vows and be resolved to work out our differences — understanding our shortcomings.

We always knew that girls grow up faster than boys. It is scientifically true. They even begin walking earlier than boys, and they mature faster. It should not surprise us that this faster development also happens even in a relationship.

A good friend of mine once told me that marriage is a work in progress. How true these words.

So ladies, if you are not being abused in any way, deprived materially or spiritually, give your man a chance to grow, so he can appreciate his relationship with you. Like mom, don't give up. Fight to keep your marriage for God hates a divorce. In most cases, you will get that phone call from your husband to tell you how much he loves you, and needs you in his life, and how he could not have done it without you. I know it can be very frustrating. Yet, the easy way out is to call it quits. But you may be giving up on your soul mate. You just don't know it because you may be choosing to end the relationship before it blossoms. Always remember, behind a successful man is a great woman. You are that individual. You are the key to a successful marriage. With God in your marriage, you can never fail.

For together, you will make a threefold bond that's unbreakable. So, take the nurturing process for what it is. Call it culture. Call it bonding. Call it being spoiled — something that happens a lot in a boy's life growing up. I am not saying it's good or bad.

It certainly makes it a little harder when we get married. But in the end, who are we to say what works and doesn't work. Not even the experts get it right all the time. Just remember, women are amazing so love them, and respect and cherish them, as much as you can.

CHAPTER 2
Idiosyncrasies

There are many things we do and say in a martial relationship that drives our wives and us up the wall and it seems that we continue to do them despite our best efforts. I have always believed that for the most part all of us are in the same boat with a few exceptions. All of us complain about the same things with seeming no hope in sight. My explanation is a simple one: you can blame the situations on imperfections or perhaps you can see it my way. I truly feel the idiosyncrasies are essential in any relationship for they allow us to manifest and cultivate qualities that are vital to a long lasting relationship — qualities such as patience, long suffering, self control, and endurance, just to name a few.

Enjoy these examples:

1.   The first one and perhaps among the top favorites is when our wives ask us to get an item in the house (pantry, closet, garage, etc.) and, of course, we can never find it. Then, of course, come the famous words uttered: "You are not looking. I bet you if I go, I will find it right away." For the most part, they do.

There is, however, a simple explanation for this remarkable occurrence. The fact is that men are single-minded creatures (one track minds). The reason we fail to find the item is that in reality we never heard our mates tell us where the item is because our minds are focused on what we were doing or thinking before being interrupted. We were already contemplating what to look for but we don't know, so we end up saying we can't find it. Now, whether you believe it or not, we do actually try hard to find the item while at the same time trying to remember the item. It's so complicated. The worst part of it is the walk back without the item. It's stressful. To make matters worse, you know she will find it. This cruel ritual can go on forever in a relationship. My solution is for us men to carry a little notepad and write down information to help us find the item.

2. We men, for some reason, hate to ask for directions. We are convinced we are going the right way. However, our wives know otherwise and they patiently implore us to ask for directions. Of course, we just say this has to be the way and we pass by many gas stations to the dismay of our dear wives. We continue to ignore the fact that there is a good possibility that we are lost. An hour later and needing fuel, we decide to listen to our wives' plea to ask for directions. I have to hand it to women, they for the most part patiently wait until we decide to ask for directions. Yet, I know they laugh at us within themselves.

We have no excuse for this bad habit of ours. Perhaps stubbornness comes into play or just a spike in testosterone is to blame or just plain stupidity. Whatever way, it drives our mates up the wall.

I do have good news though. We do grow out of this as we get older. I now get directions as soon as my wife gives me a friendly reminder that perhaps it may be a good idea to get directions. I immediately comply because after so many years of being wrong, it has dawned on me that perhaps I should listen to my wife. So, listen up guys at the first sign of feeling that you are lost. Swallow your pride and ask for directions. Take it from me, everybody will be happier.

3.   Trimming our mustaches or nose hairs is not in itself a problem. Many would agree this is a good grooming practice and something we men should routinely do. The problem comes when we do it over the bathroom sink and do not clean up after ourselves. The hair on the sink unbeknownst to us causes great vexation to our dear wives. We for our part don't even notice this until it is brought to our attention. This too will get better as time goes on, for if not, your mates will continue to remind you of the problem and eventually you will realize how much easier it is to just clean up after yourself. Unless you are the type that likes to hear his wife constantly complaining about the same issue, remember women are relentless when something is annoying them, especially when it has to do with the home. Or you could do what I did and cut off your mustache and their goes half the problem. I am a genius.

4.   The toilet seat left up is another dreaded issue. The question is who said it had to be down in the first place? It was after all created by a man in 1596 by the name of John Harrington. And no it wasn't Thomas Crapper that's a myth. This will forever be a topic of discussion with friends and a constant thorn to the women in the world, including our dear wives. The reality is that we get the short end of the stick. For if we leave the seat up, we get a mouthful. However, leaving the seat down can also cause problems if we do not wipe it off after use. So, either way, there is a good chance that our wives will get on us. The solution, I believe, is for everyone to have a share in putting the seat up or down. Just think of the time and energy that would

save. If, instead of complaining about the seat all your life with your husband or sons, all you do is when you use it, put the seat down, and when your husband uses it, he puts the seat up, resulting in a wonderfully peaceful home. Now, the ultimate solution, if you can afford it, is to build a home with his and hers toilets. Problem solved.

5.   This next point reminds me of Barney the purple dinosaur when he sang his songs about "clean up, clean up everybody, everywhere." The fact is that this point leads us to many of our wonderful discussions with our dear wives. Kind of reminds you when your mom would get on your case for not keeping your room neat and clean. It takes us a long time to grow out of this male problem. It just seems we like to leave our things around, especially in our bedrooms. I have the bad habit of leaving my shoes by the bedroom door As a man, all of us have a certain article of clothing that we tend to place down and forget about until it's too late and the wife constantly reminds us of this seeming bad habit of ours. But in my research, I asked men of different countries. I learned this problem exist in all cultures and countries. We men from youth don't worry about how are rooms look. To us, it's a haven to watch TV and sleep and just relax, until mom comes in and gives us static about our room.

I don't know if you've noticed but this is an ongoing problem that really never ends, so it seems. So why ruin a wonderful relationship because of it? I encourage wives to be like mom and put up with us and continue to remind us of the need to keep our rooms clean yet still shower us with love. We for our part as men should continue to make an effort to help out around the house, especially in the loving den. You wives instead of making it an issue and causing static in the relationship, maybe once in a while, just pick up the item and try to be understanding to our problem because we really try. Trust me, we'd rather pickup our clothes a million times over than continue to be lectured by our dear wives. Yet we don't. So my only conclusion is that this is an inherited problem we have as imperfect humans. Perhaps Adam had this issue with Eve. I don't know. I do know that this problem leads to many arguments and at times strains relationships. Love should help us overcome any problems we have. So guys, just pick up after yourselves, and make an effort. It will go a long way in your relationship.

6.   Have you ever noticed and then wondered why it is that our loving wives want to talk to us about something or anything important to them at the most awkward times. For example, two minutes to go in a football game when your team needs to win the game with a touchdown or field goal, or perhaps you are watching the end of a movie, a good movie at that, or the most popular one is when you are tired and you are about to go to sleep and she wants to talk about the end of the world.

Now, of course, I'm not saying that what's on their minds is not important. We really should listen to them. It just seems to get us in lots of trouble when we don't understand why it happens during the most awkward time. And the minute we try to explain our situation, they read it as if we don't care about them or their problem. This is not the case. We do care. It's just not the right time.

See, unless we are sick, or we are looking for an article of clothing — which in most cases was arranged or put away by our mates — we as men tend to leave them alone. It's rare that a man goes to his wife and says "honey, can we talk?"

The good news is that modern technology has almost solved this problem. For now we have TIVO which allows us to pause our program and come right back where we left off. How awesome is that. The only time it doesn't help is when you are tired. Well, we can't have it all. Guys, suck it up and just listen.

See, us men can have an argument with our wives and go to sleep without a problem, thinking that the next day everything is going to be ok. Well, women are different. When they have something on their minds, they need to talk about it right then or else they cannot function. It's the nature of their being. They are emotional creatures. That's why we love them. Yet, at times they can be a pain in your butt.

So, it's important that even though we lack understanding of this phenomenon, we need to take the time to talk to our wives to see what it is that's troubling them. Only then can we have a loving and peaceful home. Gentlemen, there is nothing in the world more wonderful than to come to a home where there is tranquility and rest.

7.   Now, this one my wife hates. It's her pet peeve. I tend to get something to drink and put back the bottle or carton of juice almost empty. So, when she gets the drink, of course, I get an ear full. Now, granted I do admit it's a bad habit and I emphasize habit because I don't do it on purpose. I'm sure most guys feel the same. Why would we want to irate our mates? It just gives us grief. We just don't think about it. Again, I believe this issue is attributed to us being single-minded creatures. So, we get what we wanted and then we proceed to put it back, not even realizing it's almost empty.

For believe me, it would be a lot easier to just finish it off and throw it away rather than to constantly hear our wives give us a speech. It would be cool, if we invented bottles or cartons that could let us know its level and when it's time to refill or throw away.

8.   Miscommunication, perhaps, gets us men in as much trouble as anything else in a man's life. We have all been there perhaps when our wives give us instructions or information concerning an issue that's important to them. For whatever reason, we just were not listening and we failed to follow through or we just completely do the opposite, or even worst, we forget. Of course, being the creatures we are, who hate to be wrong, blaming it on machismo, we swear that's it not what we heard. This could at times bring about many marital problems. They feel that we are not listening to them when they speak and this they hate with a passion. This is and will continue to be, an issue in relationships of any kind. It becomes harder if we have children, especially boys, because now the problem is magnified with the children and this brings added stress to our mates. According to them now, nobody is listening and, of course, we are to blame because children are following our bad examples.

Considering how much women have to do, we should be somewhat understanding to this dilemma.

The solution is we must pay close attention and make an earnest effort to listen. Then, we must make sure to repeat instructions back to them so we are certain as to what needs to get accomplished. Like school, we need to ask added questions if we do not understand what needs to be done. If the problem is really causing marital strain, you many consider buying a recorder or taking down notes. Remember, when all else fails, just apologize. An answer when mild turns away rage, says a wise Biblical adage. This normally does the trick, and is a lot better than a back and forth argument as to who was wrong. Two right people never accomplish much and, most of the time, these are not life and death matters. Save your arguments or discussion for issues that are important or worth discussing.

This one drives us husbands mad. Well, it does me. My wife never remembers when she has my keys, especially the car keys. Of course, she says I never gave her the keys and the discussion begins. Both of us swear the other one has them. You definitely know you don't have the keys because you know for sure that you gave them to your wife.

The problem is when they attempt to find the keys in their large purses that seem to be getting bigger and bigger, it takes them forever to search and they automatically conclude they do not have them. When in reality, they are in there along with the kitchen sink. Eventually, they find the keys and change the subject. We are normally fine with that because, unlike women, we do not like long discussions. Yet, others may say that we placed the keys there and did not tell them about it. All we can do to keep the peace is just nod our heads back and forth. In the end, it's just about keys.

9.   Two words that you will be able to relate to quickly as a problem are: dirty dishes. Dirty dishes have always been a topic of discussion among wives and a sure reason for wives to nag their husbands. I would have to agree, washing dishes is not one of our strong points. So thank God for dish washers for those of us privileged to have one. Now, if you don't have one, well we feel for you. My advice is to suck it up and help

out with the dishes from time to time. Remember that they still have to be put away and reloaded. So, your problem at times is not completely gone but life is much happier. Here are a few ways to handle this scenario to avoid unnecessary marital problems. The first and logical solution is to purchase paper plates and cups. The second is to wash or put your dishes in the dish washer as soon as you are done using them. This will prevent dishes from accumulating in the sink and drastically reduce the number of times wives get upset. Out of sight, out of mind. The third is to save the money to buy a dish washer. It pays for itself in the long run both financially and mentally.

You know, when you think about it, it's only fair for our wonderful wives who cook a good meal that can take hours that husbands should in turn help clean-up afterward. This way, both of you have time to be together to spend time watching TV or doing something that you both enjoy. If not, one of you is always tired and that can ruin a nice night, if you know what I mean.

10. This one drives me mad and perhaps some of you guys can relate. The good thing is that most of the time we drive our wives mad — a testimony of how great women are. Nevertheless, here is one. Women as a whole have no sense of time. Being late doesn't faze them as much as it bothers us. I happen to be a timely person whereas my wife is quite the opposite. Now, of course, she will deny this. Yet, more often than not, I am always rushing to many different events in my life and this drives me up the wall. It never fails, especially when we are going to a movie, a Broadway play, and sports events. We find ourselves rushing or sometimes late. I do acknowledge that we need more time to get ready. Yet, we appreciate going out with our beautiful looking and nicely

dressed wives and to them this definitely takes priority. However, for many of us, this is a problem and it causes some strain in the relationships. Patience and self-control are two excellent qualities to cultivate to help us cope. Also remember, unless it's a life and death matter, keep things in perspective. Getting angry is not going to get you there any sooner. It is only going to make matters worse for as imperfect humans we are bound to say something we don't mean and will regret saying it later. So, if possible, let your mate know ahead of time certain events that are important to you and perhaps she can be understanding to your cause and make an effort to get there on time. If all else fails, remember the saying: better late than never. So go with the flow and make the best of the situation. Why ruin a great day. Remember, though, that this doesn't work with airline flights.

11. Now, this one perhaps all of you men whose mothers threw away your old baseball cards, unknowing to them of how valuable they would be in the future, can relate: my mom threw away my cards. However, this point is not about baseball cards. It's about all the items that the women in our lives have thrown away or sold in a garage sale that to us had great value. It kind of reminds you of the joke about the husband who came home and saw that his wife was having a garage sale. She said: "Honey, you have to admit, we have a lot of junk in the house and the extra money will help some." Women have a way of convincing us to agree with them. He said: "I guess you right, dear, but I notice that all those items belong to me." Ha! Ha! Ha! So remember, if you are missing something, your wife will try to convince you that you either lost it or misplaced it. The truth is, she probably threw it away or sold it in a garage sale. To help you avoid future disappearances and marital problems, remember the phases in their lives. For example, you have seen the moody time

once a month. Well, we also have a throw away phase, believe it or not. When they begin to complain that the house seems cluttered, this is your opportunity to hide your valuable items or to remind your wife to please leave your stuff alone. On a positive note, if you don't miss the item than perhaps your wife did you a favor. As long as she doesn't throw you away, I guess everything is all right.

12. Now to some, this next example might seem crazy but it drove me nuts growing up and even continues today. I do admit mom was way worse at this than my wife. Now, this example only applies to men who are served hand and foot, as others can never understand. You get served a wonderful meal and truly appreciate the hands that put it together. a You are all ready to devour your food, hungry as ever, but there is one minor problem — you are not able to eat your food. Why, you ask? There are no utensils on your plate. This to me is cruel. It's like getting into the shower without soap or going to the restroom without tissue. You feel helpless and are forced to get up or eat with your hands. This can drive any man up the wall. Now granted, it varies in degree depending on your culture. You would have to admit that if you were in a restaurant, utensils are the first items given to you and, if you are honest, it probably would upset you if your waiter forgot them. Now, I know this is a restaurant. However, the principle is the same. Mom spoiled me. I used to yell out to mom that I had no way to eat, so she would get me my utensils no matter where she was, even if she were upstairs Word of caution. Don't try this with your mates. It works the opposite. They normally tend to get upset and look at you like you must have lost your mind. And whatever you do, never and I mean never, bring up your mom's great deed. Guarantee dog house.

13. Back to our dear wives. This one they truly hate. As you know, men are not as conscious as our mates when it comes to the house and how it looks. So we tend to not have this in mind when we invite guests over. This, as you know, causes tremendous marital strain. Our wives go bunkers, being the creatures that they are, because they worry too much about what others will say. This is one reason why, despite that I like gatherings, I have them only once in a while because when I do invite friends over, I first have to literally fix everything around the house. My honey-do list becomes a book. So, in my household to avoid problems, I normally do not have guests over without asking my wife if it's ok. Woman hate surprises and you will not like a surprised woman. If you should make this mistake, make sure you don't become a tour guide for than you will truly be in the dog house.

14. Not putting the cap on the tooth paste tube, as trivial as it may seem, does find a way to irritate your wife and bring about marital friction. The simple solution, of course, is to have your own sink, and this way you will have two separate tooth paste tubes and hopefully your wife will just worry about her own. However, if this is not your case, do not despair. Both of you will just have to come to realize that it is only a cap. You will find that marriage will give you plenty of opportunity to have discussions and disagreements on more important matters. If all else fails, just put the cap back on yourself and save yourself unnecessary arguments that take a toll on your marriage over a period of time. Learn to pick your fights; a little key to a happy relationship. Now ladies, if you do not want the aggravation, get him a toothpaste dispenser.

15. Closely connected to the tooth paste cap is the tooth paste itself left on the sink. Women tend to be a lot more tidy then us, especially at the early stages of our marriage.

It was so easy for us when we were single because we normally took mom for granted and that she would always clean the sink when she cleaned the bathroom. Now, we find ourselves sharing the sink and these issues can cause problems. Some may say, how hard can it be to clean up after yourself and the logical answer is, not hard at all. The problem is that we are single-minded creatures and there is a good chance we are in a hurry or thinking about what we are going to do after we brush our teeth and we simply forget to clean the sink. Then, there is a third reason. We just need a lot of training because it is not easy to change after years of being nurtured by mom. If a couple understands this, they will have fewer arguments and more patience, which is a quality that is essential in any relationship, especially marriage.

16. This next one is somewhat gross, I have to admit. Some of us like to clip our toe nails and not sweep up afterwards. This is one bad habit that frankly we have to correct and to make matters worse, we continue do this throughout the house. This will, without question, drive our mates mad, and especially if she has just finished sweeping or vacuuming the carpet. Guys, this is something that not even I can defend. Unfortunately, I still have this bad habit. However, I have good news. The constant remainders from our mates will help. It has helped me to the point where I am somewhat conscious of picking up after myself. If there is anything that will get my wife upset, it is a dirty house. So, if we want a happy wife, gentleman, try to change this bad habit. Our ultimate goal is to make sure our wives are always happy. Not always easy, during a certain time of the month. Yet, a loving husband will nevertheless make an effort in this regard.

17. Who can forget the remote control which allows us at random to change channels at will? This small device seems

harmless to us men. In fact, without it, we men would probably go nuts. Really, we cannot watch TV without a remote control. Personally, I do not know how TV viewing was possible before, when you had to get up and turn that TV knob. Yet, this harmless device is hated by our wives when in our possession. They can't understand why it is we just cannot stay on one channel. Of course, we call it channel surfing. This seeming small issue will bring us occasional arguments but I have noticed that it fades away later on in the relationship. It may pop up once in a while, depending on how moody your mate is that day, but overall, this is one problem that couples seem to get over pretty fast in their marital life. There is one caution to all, you can never ever take the remote when your wife is watching TV, especially when she is watching the Lifetime channel. This will bring you problems. In the end, unless it's a very important — like, for example, the Super Bowl, the World Series, etc. — the loving thing to do for the sake of peace and tranquility in the home is to let your wife watch what will make her happy.

18. This problem occurs when you expect to have certain items in the pantry or home and can't find them because your wife forgot to buy them or bought another brand name. This is especially compounded, if the item is food. For example, you can't wait to get home to eat a great burger and then you realize you have no hamburger bun or perhaps you are preparing a sandwich and find out you have no mayonnaise. We have all been there and we tend to have arguments with our wives over this issue. If you are like me, you might even call your wife that instant to ask why you do not have this particular item. Here is where the problem begins because normally the wives are sorry and they tell us that they forgot, and then they say they have too many

things to remember and why did you not remind her more or go buy it yourself. Now, I know this drives us men up the wall. The solution is simple. No need to make matters worse by asking your wife why she forgot to get the item. In all fairness to them, the grocery list may be long depending on the size of the family. And keep in mind that a woman's work is never done. Besides the groceries, they have other things on their minds. To avoid this problem, simply go grocery shopping with your mate and make a list of the things you may want and put them in the cart yourself. Now this issue is solved. This simple solution has another benefit in that it provides a wonderful opportunity to spend time with our mates and appreciate all they do for us.

19. Last but not lease is nagging. It is the word we use to describe our wives playfully and at times realistically. However, I have learned that wives, with a few exceptions, nag because many of us procrastinate or fail to accomplish our responsibilities at home. An example, is the honey-do list. We have had the list for two years and therefore our wives find themselves reminding us often and we interpret these reminders as nags. In reality, these may be important reminders for the family. Women are a lot more organized than we are and because of this, they are good in buying time to take care of matters in the household. I have found that if we make a list such as the infamous honey-do list, we will accomplish more and have fewer arguments at home. Then, the nagging will diminish and the home will become a peaceful haven for all. So, instead of all the name calling, perhaps you might want to examine your situation and see how to remedy the problem. Listening is a wonderful quality that will go a long way in helping us to understand each other and we will begin to interpret what we once thought

was nagging to be a concern that our mates have. Now, don't miss understand me, there are woman who nag but for the most part woman just want their home to look nice. There is no sin in that, so, gentlemen, make the queen happy and take care of your list pronto.

CHAPTER 3
The Jerk

Really, who isn't one at one point in their lives? I was one of them and continue to be one from time to time. In talking to other couples, I have concluded, based on extensive research and interviews with common people, that men for the most part act likes jerks toward those they claim to love. They fail to appreciate everything that their mates do for them and for their relationship, like my wife who is the true inspiration for this book. Now before you men start knocking down my door I realize not all men are Jerks that's my disclaimer.

Another reason for writing this book is that, through my 35 years of my marriage and also the many experiences of others, there is no denying that it takes us men years to grow up and because of this immaturity, we act like jerks. I truly believe that, on average, we don't mature until about 35 to 40 years of age depending on different factors we experienced growing up. The problem is that most women, unlike previous generations, don't have the patience or desire to wait. There is also another explanation for our actions that I have begun to examine that may explain the reason for us acting like jerks. Medically speaking, some of us perhaps have a clinical mental imbalance, such as being bipolar or having mental depression that we fail to acknowledge or refused to admit. We must also remember that medical conditions like being bipolar in the brain were not widely known for some time and only recently has attention been given to these severe mood swings in people. Because of this, we do not receive the needed medical attention to help us control our emotions. Men for some reason hate to go see a doctor. Their testosterone levels make them feel that everything is all right and they have no problems — it's just that others do not understand them. Without this help, the marriage suffers and the burden falls on those we love.

This is what happened to me for many years. I gave my wife a hard time acting like a jerk on many occasions. I said and did things that hurt the one person who truly deserved better. This is something that will forever be on my conscience and now I regret it every day of my life. I could never bring back the past but my past could help me and others to make the future better. My goal now is to love, respect, and appreciate my wife as much and as often as possible. I am blessed to have a loving wife committed to our marriage. Love for God was no doubt a big reason why my wife put up with me all these years. No doubt you can look back at your relationship and, if it's not too late, make the needed adjustments to strengthen your bond with each other. If currently you are a jerk, hopefully, you will finish this book and then you will truly understand what it means to love and admire your woman.

Women as a group have the ability, perhaps due to their inherited maternal instinct, to be more understanding and patient with us than men are with them. This helps them to a certain degree to put up with our immature ways and this could go on for years. They make repeated efforts to appeal to us through kindness, love, and other forms of expression common in woman. Some of us are moved to change for the better. However, some of us continue to act like jerks despite their efforts. There are times we catch ourselves. We feel bad so we apologize. We say "I'm sorry" or utter the words made famous by us men, "I promise it won't happen again. I promise to change." This normally may last a day or at most a few days before we act like jerks again, saying or doing things that hurt the one we love. Fortunately for us, God created flowers. Flowers have the ability to get us out of the dog house on many occasions. But, I really do not think God created flowers for this purpose because God created the first man and woman perfect. Adam never acted like a jerk. Giving flowers then is actually a way that we can show our appreciation and love toward our mates any time we want to express ourselves to them. Unfortunately, though, due to our imperfection, flowers tend to be given only if it's Valentine's Day, or when we have done or said something wrong. The funny thing is that flowers mean so much more when we give them out of pure appreciation and just plain old love.

It broke my heart to see my wife cry because of the stupid things I said and did. And, perhaps, many of us men can relate to this. Yet, the troubling part is that we continue to do this and sometimes we hate ourselves for being this way. We want to make the needed changes in our relationships so we can stop but it's not always easy. Sometimes, it seems this is a growing process we men go through, or have to grow through, in order to appreciate others, especially those we love.

Now, the reason why I say this is not in any way to excuse our behavior. It may give us clues as to why we are the way we are and this goes back to my first chapter on nurturing and how a young boy grows up. It wasn't until I saw my own son interact with his mother that I began to see confirmation of my theory. Young boys as they get older, but not so much in young years as during adolescence, begin during teenage to develop male dominate traits and, of course, they seem to develop these traits with their mothers. I started noticing this when my wife and son would begin to have argumentative discussions with each other. It seemed that this was a daily occurrence over practically everything. At first, it would drive me crazy. I would ask my wife why she argues with my son. I would tell my wife that she was the mother and that she should just set the rules and avoid lengthy discussions with him. Of course, at times, he would say things that were hurtful to his mother and, yet more often than not, they would be very affectionate with each other. My son would even worry about his mother if she were running late on getting home. At times, he seemed to be more concerned than even I was. This behavior continues until they begin to appreciate their mothers.

On my part, I would argue with my wife about why she seems to be allowing this kind of behavior. She would complain to me about it, and yet, she continued to argue with Ryan and again complain to me. Perhaps you men can relate. This behavior goes back to my chapter on nurturing because in the end young men go through a stage in life where they are bonding with their mothers through this process of having confrontations with them. Eventually, they grow up to love them dearly in most cases. They often get married and follow the same pattern with their wives. My theory is that this is all they know. It may seem hard to understand why we act this way or why we need to go through this process to get close to our mates. I'm sure this is not how God intended relationships to be. However, being imperfect humans at times insures that our behaviors are hard to explain or understand. Yet, in talking to other couples, especially the wives, it seems many of us go through this process. Unfortunately though, unlike our beautiful mothers who for the most part never gave up on their children, this is not the case with all wives — that's just their maternal instinct that kicks in. I'm not denying the fact that most men are jerks until they grow up and begin to appreciate their mates. I do have compassion for what many women go through. Some wives may never say that they have good reason for leaving their husbands and I am not in a position to judge them on the decision they have taken. However, we must remember that vows were exchanged between two individuals before God. Marriage is sacred in His eyes and divorce should not be an option unless it is scriptural. Both parties should iron out their differences and fight to keep their marriage going. You can take the easy way out and get a divorce for under $200 dollars. It's like ordering a divorce through the mail. Marriage is a work in progress, a good friend of mine once told me. I'm so happy I listened to him. I am also grateful to my wife for being loyal to her vows and allowing our marriage to grow to what it is today. It's not perfect but nothing is in life. Couples, you have to give your relationship a chance to work. Giving up is easy. Yes, I agree that many men are just jerks. They act the same way with their own mothers so don't take it personally. We all go through this process but, eventually, many of us get our act together and we grow up to be loving husbands. It takes a pearl thousands of years to become the beautiful gem so many woman love. Yet, it is through a process of continued friction that it gets to become a pearl. Marriage or any relationship is the same; give it a chance and see for yourself how it will blossom.

CHAPTER 4
The Beginning

When Adam first saw Eve he uttered the first pickup line in human relationships: "At last, bone of my bone, flesh of my flesh." Beautiful words indeed back in those days from a man who just saw the love of his life. This was also the first recorded instance of love at first sight. I could only imagine how beautiful Eve must have been. How thankful Adam was to have a companion — someone he could talk to, someone he could do things with, and someone he could express his love to.

When you think about it, in one way or another, this is how most relationships begin. We all have an individual story all very special and unique to each couple. The common denominator is that we fall in love. Mine was not at first sight even though my wife is beautiful. For me, it happened later on. I met the love of my life and future wife at a pizza joint. Two weeks later, we went on our first date and the rest is another story.

So what I want to discuss is how we can as men bottle this moment so we can appreciate our wives and give them the attention and love they deserve. To help you, I make this list of what woman do that make them amazing creatures.

Now granted, they have their moments but we would too if we went through one-third of what they go through physically and emotionally — especially during the monthly visit of their "friend," if you understand what I mean. Even though it becomes a challenge for us as men, it's an experience we simply can't initially comprehend. When you think what it was when mom went through it, she took it out on dad and we thought she was just having a bad day. If you had a sister, you thought she was being mean to you that day. Who knew as a kid? I didn't. Yet, we understood and continued to grow up with our families and loved them. The good thing is that it does get better as marriage goes on, only if through our maturity we begin to understand and show companionship and kindness to our mates.

Eve was created as a complement to Adam. She would be his helper, number one supporter, and best friend. The Bible says that they would become as one for they had one purpose — to worship the Creator and to love one another. Together they would form a happy family with Eve taking on a major role in the success of her family. There is a saying — behind a good husband is a great and amazing wife.

Take note of all the things women do. They are endearing persons who truly love and care about their family. Sometime ago, an article came out that showed all the things women do in a family and estimated that their salary would be about $263,000 a year for doing those things. It listed all the positions they have in the family circle. All the hats they wear clearly shows why women are amazing. Long before this article, God in his word the Bible spoke of a proverbial wife at Proverbs 31. If you read this passage in your Bible, you will get a true appreciation for women and how vital a role they have in the family.

These are some ways, in no particular order, that will show how amazing women are and just a few reasons why we should appreciate and love them.

1. You have a personal nurse. Most nurses do a wonderful job but this woman is not just any ordinary nurse. She truly

has your best interest in mind because this nurse loves you, and cares for you. She is by your side until you get better. And you know how baby we get as men when we get sick. Yet, time and again, our dear wives are there to take care of us. To make us a nice soup or a hot tea or give us our medicine — whatever the case — our nurse is always there for us. We don't have to press a button to receive help. They naturally always make many visits to see how we are doing and we get a kiss on the forehead from time to time. Gentlemen, we must appreciate these loving gestures from those who love us.

2.   Women are in general the best administrators of the household. In my case, my wife handles all my financial affairs and I never worry about my money for I truly trust her with my finances. Just a word of caution. You have to make sure that if you choose this course, it's imperative that your mate is financially responsible with the funds in the family. Of course, this at times may add extra stress to your dear wives. However, they do it because they know that it will help the family. They also manage the kitchen expenses, making sure the family is well nourished and the pantry is full with the items needed to keep the children happy and the husband satisfied. And all we have to do, at least in my case, is accompany my wife, whenever I can, to the supermarket, pushing the cart as she systematically purchases without a list all of the foods that make everyone at home happy and full. These two things should instill in us appreciation for what most women do. We must continue.

3.   Women have an incredible way of knowing when things are not right. I never truly understood why my mother would often say to me: "Listen to your mother." You can say they have a sixth sense about this that most of the times, when we fail

to heed their advice, things normally do not go good. This I eventually figured out from my mother and the experiences I went through and now from my wife. Unlike women, us men are quick to action and decisions. We don't always see the whole picture as it were. We don't see the consequences of our actions. Women on the other hand are able to think things out, look ahead, see all the angles and this allows them to make better decisions. They have the ability to see danger and the forethought to understand what may happen if a certain course is taken. We just don't have those skills and if we do, our macho always seems to get in the way. The key is for us to be humble enough to listen to them and consider their ideas, suggestion, and thoughts. Who needs PhDs? Our dear wives could be our best advisors, counselors, and even teachers in our family. They have a maternal insight that we do not have that makes them truly amazing. So listen to them and give them undivided attention when they speak to us. To paraphrase the old EF Hutton commercials— when wives speak, everyone stop whatever they are doing and listen. We should do the same for these women if we want what is best for us.

4.   In my case, my wife is also my tailor. Some of you men can relate. For I do not buy any clothes for myself. My wife literally buys everything I wear. From my socks to my underwear to my suits and ties. Like many of you, often I get complimented for the combination of shirts and ties. I always respond by saying: "Thank you. My wife buys all my clothes." Women do not get enough credit when it comes to their mate's wardrobe. If it was not for them, we would have nothing to wear and if we selected our clothes, we would not look as good as we do. Our personal designer and we don't even know it. We take it for granted. It all goes back to my first chapter about when your nurturing mom bought you all your clothes, dressed you, and

combed your hair, and now your wife does the same. OK, we can exempt combing your hair. So you see, gentlemen, this is why they deserve better. So, the next time someone gives you a compliment, tell them thank you and then give your wife all the credit. Let your wife dress you and you will always look good. Remember what Deion Sanders says — you are what you wear. And, if you want to be successful in anything in life, you need to start by looking good.

5.   Now, this is my favorite. My wife is also a chef and this is to me her greatest asset. They say the way to get to a man's heart is through his belly. Most woman learn to be great cooks just so they can satisfy their husbands and next their children. They call their mom or friends, if they need to learn a certain recipe, just so they can cook a good meal for the family. Since I am of Latin decent, my wife would call my mother to learn Spanish dishes to make my marital transition easier. She has become a great cook. They truly take pleasure and delight in seeing their family enjoy dinner. I can still recall my beautiful wife calling my mom to ask for recipes of foods I like. How endearing an act this is. We should never compare our mothers cooking to our mates. This is something often done by men, myself included, especially early in our marriage. Just remember mom did not start off a great chef. She probably did the same when she first got married. Recall that initially in your relationship with mom, she gave you food in a jar. What makes women great is that they try and eventually they truly become awesome chefs. Another tip is to eat whatever is given to you. This is important early in your marriage. However, be honest with her so she can make it better or stop making it altogether. But always appreciate the effort.

6.   Housewife/maid work some men don't realize how much work this entails. The foolish man would want you to believe

that a housewife just stays home, goes to the gym, and shops all day. And when she is not doing all that, she is watching soap operas all afternoon. That may be true in Hollywood or with the rich and famous but in general a typical housewife is far from that. This I learned the first time I stayed home to take care of my daughter. It took me only an hour to realize how much work it takes to take care of a home. I recommend every man who is taking their mates for granted to switch places for just one day and see how valuable your wife is to the family. A housewife not only takes care of the child, which includes playing, feeding, and teaching the child — which for us men is a full day of work, yet at the same time, they cook, clean house, wash clothes, iron clothes, do errands, and go to appointments. If you have kids, then it is pickup kids from school and even home school, and the list goes on. Gentlemen, trust me when I tell you that you do not want to switch places. Instead, let them know how much you love them and realize how hard they work and show your appreciation for their true qualities and desires. It's an amazing thing to see them at work. All we can do is admire them and make their job easier by picking up after ourselves from time to time and not creating more work for them. If a tired wife needs to rest, it leaves no time for us to enjoy the other benefits of marriage, if you know what I mean.

So you see, need I say more. Woman are deserving of our undivided love and attention. For some reason, as time goes on, we begin to take them for granted. The love we had at first for them begins to fade. We begin to treat them differently, even with unkind words or thoughtless acts. Yet, this chapter reminds us of all they do and the reasons we should appreciate them. But now, our love and care for them is not based on how much they do, it's based on why they do it. Women play an integral role in the success of a family. They are a complement to what makes everyday life run smoothly in a family. They are the reason why a spiritual man works hard to provide for his family. You can see why Adam when he saw Eve said — at last bone of my bone, flesh of my flesh. If you have this precious wife in your wonderful midst, cherish her, love her, and take care of her because this gem is hard to find and whenever you do, do everything in your power to never to lose her.

CHAPTER 5
The Affair

When God created Adam and Eve, He instituted the family arrangement of a husband and wife. He said a man will leave his mother and his father and he must stick to his wife and they will become one. One in purpose. One in thought. Together, they would produce a perfect a family, extending the Garden of Eden to every corner of the earth. The first happy family. But we all know something went wrong. Selfishness crept into the first human family, starting with Eve. With that came sin. The reason why this is so important is because I believe that selfishness, yes selfishness, is the root cause for the most destructive, the most painful thing, we can do in our marriage.

To have an affair is to be unfaithful, and disloyal in your marriage. They say besides death itself, it is the most devastating feeling one goes through when a mate has an affair. I could not tell you how it feels because I have personally never have had to undergo such pain. However, I have seen it's affects on others from strangers who related their experience to me to very close friends of mine who I have loved dearly. From what I have seen, it is truly a sad thing to see. To satisfy an initially selfish desire, lives are destroyed, families torn apart, and friendship gone. Yes, it's that simple.

Its roots begin with selfishness for how can you explain forgetting about all those who love you and everything you gave to a relationship for a desire to have sex with someone else?

I have been happily married for 35 years. Has it been easy? No. It's been hard at times. There is no doubt that marriage is a work in progress. And it's seems like the older we get, the more we argue about everything. That's another book in itself that I may write in the future. Yet, I believe there is no excuse for infidelity and hopefully you will never subject the one you love to this horrible deathlike feeling. Yes, people will justify just about anything to make themselves feel better as to why they are committing this terrible thing on those they love. Let me try to rationalize their thinking, so you can perhaps prevent such stupidity and foolish thinking in your life and spare you from committing a mistake that you may regret and maybe not fix.

People have all kinds of reasons to commit such an act.

1. The so-called educated, who believe we descended from apes, would have us believe that this is quite normal for we have been programmed to breed and to do this we need many partners. So, how could you fault men for such a act when all they are doing is carry out their instinctive behavior that is what an animal would do? Can this animalistic reasoning truly bring comfort to a victim of infidelity? Yea, right. I guess that's where the phrase came out — what an animal! You can continue to believe this foolish theory from the so-called educated and continue to see the destruction of the family circle and by extension, the demise of society itself. Life has a purpose and it's not to believe that we should have no regard for how we act and who we hurt, just to fulfill an immoral desire to satisfy a wrong feeling that many of us get because of imperfection and bad thoughts. We are not animals who act on extinct. We were created with a conscience. We have the ability to say no, to think before we act, and to act on what is right. We have morals and a need to worship someone. Animals do not have this ability.

2. True, they are those who believe this psychological babble to explain or not explain their behaviors. They actually tell you how often they try to reason with themselves not to throw everything away and that they do not know why they are acting this way. They even go as far as seeing a professional throughout their affair to help them understand and explain why they chose such a destructive course in life. The funny thing is that just like habitual gamblers, or drunks, they eventually believe their own lies. These folks truly convince themselves that something must be wrong with them for what other explanation can they truly give for such a behavior. Well, if you find yourself in this group, let me save you some money. There is nothing wrong with you psychologically. If you search your heart, you will see exactly why you are having an affair. The answer is simple. You do this because of selfishness. The fact is that you are a selfish person. Think about it. To disrespect everyone else in your life, even the one you say you love, all to satisfy your immoral desires, is the ultimate act of selfishness. So, stop kidding yourself by blaming your brain because it's not psychological. It's your heart. The Bible says the heart is treacherous. Who can know it? It's obvious you don't. So, do us all favor and stop using the word love so often to those you are hurting. You are not crazy. You are just plain selfish, and you know it.

3. Now granted, there may be situations in a relationship that one may justify having an affair due to mental or physical abuse. In some cases, they find someone who treats them totally the opposite. Someone who gives them attention and tells them everything they want to hear. This includes women and men. So, they naturally begin to feel needed and wanted, and they gravitate toward the individual who is giving them all this attention — especially if they feel worthless because

of all the abuse. Yet, in this extreme case, the solution is not to have an affair. Let me explain why.

Two wrongs don't make a right. Yes, no one should be abused, and yes, you deserve to be treated in a better way. However, the act of infidelity is not just against your husband, but also against God who has never been disloyal to you. Remember, you are being selfish. Your actions can hurt others, your conscience, and damage your mind and heart. So, if you do find somebody who truly cares for you and is not just another jerk that is also using you — which, in most cases, happens and you get into another abusive relationship. Perhaps you can separate, or get a divorce. So, in the end, do the right thing for only this can truly make you feel good about yourself.

4.   Then, there are the fools who say they love their mates and will not leave them for someone else, and normally cry like babies when they are caught. Well, these individuals just want to have someone on the side with no strings attached. They believe that as long as you love your mate and take care of your family there is nothing wrong in having an affair. I guess, in the case of a man, it's a macho thing. In fact, in some countries, it's viewed as normal. In a country like Ecuador, 78% of men have affairs and the incredible part is the women know this. They obviously don't like it but many have nowhere to go. They do it for their children, and because they feel that it is culturally accepted, they stay with their unfaithful mates. So, the end result is that people continue to behave this way, rationalizing that everything is all right. Of course, in Western societies, this is changing for women are catching up to the men.

5.   This reason, because of not being strong-minded, actually gets many baited into adulterous relationships. This person is weak- minded and allows his pure confidence to deceive him.

Yes, this person also lacks loyalty, like most of the scenarios I discuss. Is this an excuse? Absolutely not. I'm in no way or fashion condoning him or her for such actions. I am just making the point that these individuals get lured into a relationship and before they know it, it is too late. A good example of this is when you go to the beach. No doubt this has happened to you as you are swimming or playing around, you begin to stray and you will not know until you realize how far you have strayed. How easy it is to get into this scenario. It is as simple as flirting with the opposite sex in what may seem innocent but is very dangerous for the attention blinds you. Eventually, you go into the next step — going out just for a fun happy hour and after a few drinks, then it's on to the person's house for some coffee. You know the end of this movie. The mind is a terrible thing to waste. It should be telling you, don't go there, don't be a fool, look out, see the full picture. But you can't because you are not a strong-minded person, and eventually you succumb to your weakness. And then, you will try to rationalize how this happened to you. You can't even explain it, yet, you try to over and over again. You try to understand how this happened to you. Do yourself a favor. Stop trying and start working on your determination to remain loyal to your spouse. The heart is treacherous so don't trust it. However, your mind you can control if you fill it with righteous principles. See, when you are at your weakest point, your mind is the only thing working as you begin to ponder on what is going on, and believe me you will ponder. If you have nothing in your mind to draw from that is good, and you have a weak mind, well, your fleshly desires will eventually overcome you, and then you fall victim to this trap. However, if you are a man of principles and can draw from such qualities as love, loyalty, and self-control, you will be successful. You will see the end of this movie. Will it be a love story or a horror movie with you ending up being killed by the monster. You get the point.

6.   Last but not least is the one who gets drunk and wakes up in bed with someone else not his mate next to him. They have even made movies about this scenario. It happens more than you think. You jump out of bed wondering who in the world that person in the bed is. Then, it hits you like a brick and you pray and hope nothing happened. But it did. Flashes of your wife or husband or children go through your mind. This must be a horrible feeling. I can't really help out in this regard because, thank God, I have never been through this experience. I just know from others' experiences and movies — your life literally turns upside down. In the distance, you can hear the song "Blame it On the Bottle." This is no joking matter. You can lose your family for one act of stupidity, all because you did not control your drinking and you put yourself in a situation perhaps you should have not been in. My rule is I never go anywhere without my wife, especially if there is going to be other woman and alcohol in the same room. I am also a strong believer against girls' night out. You should hear the stories. Sorry folks, call me a male chauvinist if you want but in my home this does not work. I also abide by the same rule. What's good for the goose is good for the gander. Now before you get all bend out of shape Yes I trust my wife and Yes there is nothing wrong in your love ones both husband and wives going out with their friends from time to time to places where they can enjoy each others company I'm just saying that going out to places where men and women go to pick up people perhaps is not the best place to go if you are married and there is drinking involved. Like I said you should hear the stories before you get all shaken up.

Getting back to this scenario that you have just committed adultery with someone you do not even know. What do you tell your mate? What possible explanation do you have? You have none. Just come clean and beg for forgiveness, and maybe you have a chance. Lying about your problem will not help. It will only get worst. Throw yourself on the mercy of your spouse. Drunk or not, you were still disloyal. My motto is that there are no excuses for being unfaithful.

CHAPTER 6
True Love — Also Known As Soul Mate

This is the ultimate form of love from a relationship standpoint. Of course, there are other forms of love, such as Agape, and Philia, and Eros. However, this love is the one everyone feels when they believe they have found the "one." You know: this is the one; we were made for each other. No doubt you have heard such expressions before. Let me say, I am a believer of true love. I will later explain in detail the real meaning of true love and not the Hollywood version.

I first learned of this phrase in the movie, *"The Princess Bride"* — a wonderful love story which, by the way, I highly recommend. In it, Wesley and Buttercup fall in love. His love for her is unbreakable. He goes to the end of the earth to save her. The movie, in a funny way, shows the extent of his love for his Buttercup and there is a scene in the movie, without giving it away, where he utters the phrase, "true love." That's the point of the movie. Their love is pure, loyal, and unbreakable — all ingredients needed to obtain true love. Other movies have also highlighted this. There is *"The Notebook,"* my favorite love story. This story, without saying it, shows the true meaning of true love. At one point in the movie, his kids come to visit him at the nursing home to encourage him to come home and leave mom. In nursing home, he says: "Guys, that's my baby. This is my home now. I can't leave her." That scene alone will bring tears to your eyes.

Of course, I can make a whole chapter on love stories. And really guys, it can't hurt you to watch love movies or, as some would say, chick movies from time to time. I use to hate these movies. Now, I enjoy them and feel they have helped me in my relationship with my wife. Try it. It's cheaper than marriage counseling.

But you know, the concept of true love existed way before Hollywood. Believe it or not, there is a Biblical account highlighting a love story of the same kind of love. It is the account of the Shepherd Boy and King Solomon and the Shulamite Maiden found in the Bible book called "The Song of Solomon." The book is actually a love song. It's truly an enchanting love story. This song tells about a beautiful country girl who preferred to marry her Shepherd companion rather than accept the offer of King Solomon to become one of his wives. Now, King Solomon employed all his wisdom and wealth to win her heart and he promised to give her all the jewelry she could imagine. He housed her in his royal home so impressive that when the Queen of Sheba saw it, she was left breathless. Yet, the girl's love for the shepherd boy could not be shaken. She remained loyal to the humble shepherd to whom she was promised in marriage. This is just a little excerpt of how she felt. She said: "Place me as a seal upon your heart, as a seal upon your arm; because love is as strong as death is…. Many waters themselves are not able to extinguish love nor can rivers themselves wash it away." Wow, that's amore.

You see, true love does exist. However, it's not based on fate or destiny. I think that God is not a matchmaker because He created us as free moral agents to choose for ourselves. Of course, I can't say that dogmatically because I don't know for sure. Yet, based on my own thought and what I have read, the person in your life will be of your choosing and desire. No, love is not blind. I know you have heard that before but the fact is that you probably had lots of alerts, warnings, speeches, and indications to tell you otherwise but you just decided to ignore them. Your eyes had nothing to do with your choice, it was all in your mind. We say "love is blind" to justify an excuse, a choice, or mates.

There are so many intangibles for the one we fall in love with; nobody can really give you a true answer. Many try or theorize or give an opinion. I guess that's why we at times shake our heads when we see couples, who look, act, and speak completely opposite of each other and we wonder how in the world did these two meet and fall in love. Yet, the minute they fall in love, any couple can reach "true love." You notice I said "reach" because true love is cultivated during a period of time. How long? It varies. One thing for sure, when you get there, you know without a shadow of a doubt that you have found your soul mate. The person in your life that you can't live without. I know this because without my wife I feel lost and at times disoriented. And when she is away for a few days because of work or visiting her mom, I feel something missing in my life. I get this nervous feeling over me that's very uncomfortable. And it goes away the second I see her again. That's why my wife doesn't go away for long periods of times. I am not a believer of girls' nights out or weekend getaways of women. I'm sorry. I don't do it so I don't let my wife do it. And yes, I trust her. It's not an insecurity issue. I just don't trust people in general. Perhaps I am being a little unreasonable and as husbands we should always trust our mates.

As I mentioned, true love is cultivated. Let me share an illustration/story that helps us to understand how we can reach true love in any relationship. God is love. His dominant quality is love for God is love. We learn so much from Him in his created works. For example, you truly do not see the beauty of a plant, flower, or tree until it fully blossoms. Then and only then, can you truly appreciate its beauty. When they blossom, they may even have color, different shapes, or have pleasant odors, and you're amazed at the transformations. Of course, this book is not about botany yet we learn that much is needed for this to take place. A true landscaper will tell you that water, nourishment, sun, care, and much more are all vital to the cultivation of a beautiful flower or plant. Without these necessary things, the flower or plant will actually wither and die.

True love is a state of feeling we all can reach with time and great effort. Marriage is a work in progress. Like so many things in life, the more we put into it, the more results we get. True love is only attainable if we are committed in fulfilling our vow until death do us part, in sickness or in health. See, those words are not to be taken lightly. They can be the reasons that help us reach the state of true love. For like the flowers or plants, cultivation is needed so the original love that bonded you together at first may grow into a love that is unbreakable — a love that is so strong that nothing or anyone can destroy; a love that only thinks about how to make the other person happy; a love that is willingly to get in front of a freight train even if it meant his/her life. This is true love.

It has taken me some time, after years of studying relationships throughout my life, to think about this book and this chapter on true love — starting with my parents, who were married 50 years as of 2012, and so many others. I met a person whose grandparents married 72 years ago. I am convinced that everyone has the potential to reach this ultimate feeling in a relationship. Now granted, there are some relationships that should never have started and are set up for failure from the beginning. All of us have come across an experience of this case at one point in our lives but, for the most part, something draws us to the person we fall in love with. It could be their smile, eyes, personality, and even their cooking. Yes, we have to have a physical attraction. That's a given. What is constant in my mind is the fact that both of you fell in love.

The minute you fell in love, you knew that you wanted to spend the rest of your life with this person. You did not entertain or ponder getting a divorce, leaving each other, or being unfaithful. That never comes into our minds in the beginning stages of our relationship when we fell in love. You are in love at this point. Everyone can reach true love. Some do and I believe I have. Based on how much my wife has done to support and keep our marriage together, there is no doubt in my mind and heart that she is my soul mate, my true love. Barry White put it best in his song, *"You're the First, the Last, My Everything."* This should be in everyone's collection of love songs, if you are truly in love.

Then comes the unexplainable. These same individuals who proclaim their love for each other, who had been married for 10, 15, 20, 25 years and more, who in some cases worked so hard to make their marriage work, who go through various challenges and heartaches together, and then one day, they decide to go their separate ways. And you ask yourself what in the world went wrong? How does this happen? I have met countless people, married as long as 25 years with grown children, who become unfaithful.

Now, in Chapter 5, I explained reasons people make for having an affair. Yet, the answer to why, still keeps me wondering and thinking and trying to rationalize this behavior. Of course, all the educated people with degrees will give you their theories and physiological explanation, yet this happens more and more often. I always wondered how a person who claims to love someone can behave this way. I think we are looking too deep for the answer. Perhaps the explanation is right in front of us. It's simple, and not at all complicated. Let me save you some money. It's obvious that all these marriage counselors are not providing satisfying answers to this dilemma. Granted, many of them have temporary solutions or bandage solutions. Few look to the origination of the family circle — to the One who married the first couple, Adam and Eve. Here lies the answer to our problem. I go back to the question. Can a person love someone and still behave this way? For many years, I thought, no they can't. I remember what the Bible says about love, so I thought love doesn't behave this way. But, as time went on, I realize something else.

Maybe, I am wrong all my life about how a person can claim to love someone while at the same time be having an affair. I reasoned that love, genuine love, could never behave this way. I wondered how you could make the claim you love one while hurting that person in every possible way mentally and emotionally and physically and even spiritually.

They say that only to death itself, infidelity ranks second in the emotional toll a person goes through. The feelings of losing someone in a figurative death. This one may even be harder to deal with because the person is still alive and you are constantly replaying in your mind the love you once had and what went wrong. The simple answer to this perplexing thought is NO. And many, especially women, will agree. Can you blame them? Women have a higher sense of loyalty and commitment to themselves and family. Emotionally, it is hard for them to accept the notion that a man who is unfaithful can still claim to love his mate. Yet, despite the fact that this chapter is about true love, I have always wondered if it is possible to love someone and commit this terrible act of disloyalty.

It has taken me many months as I considered writing this chapter, what my answer would be. I have thought about it through different angles. I rationalized all my thoughts from an emotional mindset to a spiritual one and my conclusion is YES. I believe it's possible. Let me explain.

As imperfect beings, we have the ability to love and to make mistakes at the same time. Am I using imperfection as an excuse? No. Am I condoning such actions? Yet, the fact is that humans throughout history have made horrible mistakes. However, their love is not in question. As imperfect beings, we strive to do what is good. We start off with the greatest of intentions. Motives may be sincere in nature and despite all this, we sin. There are many reasons why we fall victim to sin. We can look back after the fact and see where we went wrong, what danger signs we overlooked, and what counsel we failed to heed, and regret every moment. All this can and does happen every day to imperfect people who are in love.

I believe that love, in some cases, is not in question. The problem is that these individuals are not loyal. The two at times may not go hand-in-hand. Our imperfect state allows us, in some cases, to not work together. We may think that they should emotionally but it's hard for us to accept that they don't. However, life teaches us otherwise.

For example, we could look to historical characters to get to my conclusions.

King David of Israel committed a terrible sin. We can say he made a wrong mistake when he committed adultery with Bathsheba. Yet, who can deny his love for God? His heartfelt songs to God indicate his genuine love for his creator. This in part was a big reason why God spared his life. Now granted, some may say, that this is a different kind of love. And technically, they are right as they may be based on different ideas. Agape love is a love based on principle and Eros love is based on human qualities between two people.

The emotions, however, are the same. They both spring from the heart. In each case, one can go as far as giving his life for this person and still, on the other hand, make a mistake due to his imperfection.

And then, there are countless Individuals who commit adultery or cheat on their girlfriends or visa versa, who, I believe, still love their significant other. That is why they cry like babies to win them back. They have no intention of leaving the person they love, and if they do lose them, they will tell you how they would do anything to have them back again. In most cases, these people act in a selfish way with no consideration for the feelings of others. They are disloyal in nature without moral principles. Yet, I don't doubt that they have the capacity to still love. Perhaps, they don't understand or appreciate the true meaning of love, for if they did, they would know that love does not behave indecently.

Love never fails. True love is everlasting, if we add the quality of loyalty to it.

So, to everyone who is in love, cherish what you have. Allow the love you have to blossom into true love — something that is attainable in all relationships, if we let love grow to its potential by nurturing it, by being self sacrificing, by being unselfish in your words and actions. Sprinkle lots of self control and patience on it.

Don't be the person who ends up being alone one night regretting what you did, hoping you can get a second chance, and knowing that you have just lost the love of your life. What a horrible feeling that must be. Before you throw it all away, here are some things you should ask yourself:

1. Do you see yourself with this person in the near future?

2. Do you love this other person?

3. Is it worth it? Especially if you have children?

4.   Do you want to see someone else with your wife and raising your children?

5.   What is making you behave this way?

6.   What would your family and friends think and how would it affect them?

True love is precious. I found it and nothing in this world is worth giving it up. The love of my life is the inspiration to this book. Think about what brought you together, why you fell in love, and hold onto those moments when the storm comes. When the figurative hurricane comes into your relationship, bunker under and weather the storm. The next day, after the storm, the sky is blue, the sun is shining, and everything is calm.

Always remember my motto: "Make love not War."

CHAPTER 7
Children –
A Gift From God

Children are indeed a gift from God but they can be a royal pain in the butt at times. I have two beautiful kids, both lovable in their own way. One is shy, the other more out spoken and that's the point. No two kids are alike and this is where the challenge is in rearing children. See, what works for one child may or probably will not work with the second one. No matter how experienced you think you are in rearing children, life teaches you that when it comes to children, its like a football draft, you just don't know how the player will turn out until he starts playing with the pros. Children are the same. You can inculcate into them all the values and principles that will help him or her be an outstanding citizen and an asset to a community and/or congregation. You can instill in them a wholesome fear of God that will protect them from unwholesome vices and people and things. Yet, with all this training, in the end it is up to them to decide and make choices. No matter how hard you have tried and how many books you have read, nothing is guaranteed as to how your children will turn out. One thing is for sure, along the way you will experience problems, challenges, and some disappointments. How you handle these issues will determine your success as a parent and perhaps how your kids will turn out. Now remember, even God had children who went astray. So, don't blame yourself for your children's outcome, if you have done all you can. The key is never lower your standards, stay consistent in your decisions, and never give up.

I'm sure you have heard this a million times, if you are a parent: "It's just a stage they are going through." The funny thing is this statement is actually true. Now granted, it brings us no comfort at that moment, however, it does give us a measure of hope. So yes, you will get pass the terrible 2's, and just to let you know, the terrible 2's go into the 3's, the 4's, and sometimes, the 5's. Then come the scary years in middle school, when your lads become teenagers. Yes, the teen years. This too will also pass. By the way, drinking by parents in moderation helps during this phase.

Then come the high school years and all the drama associated with it. I always say, if your kids get pass high school, you are almost half way there. By the way, your kid's graduation is great so make sure you do not miss it. Yes, I am talking to you, dad, as these are special moments in a kid's life, so whatever you are doing, it can wait. These are the moments our kids can draw upon when they face challenges such as peer pressure, or when they feel down and out for whatever reason. They can look back and draw strength from these experiences and use these positive energies to cope or overcome whatever problems they may be facing or will face. Now let me say again, I am not a doctor, psychologist or social worker but really how many parents are. Most of us are ordinary folks just trying to raise our children the best way we know how. And for the most part, in general, parents have done a great job! See, in life, when you buy something, every product comes with a manual, except kids. And all these experts seemingly think they have all the answers and on paper, it all sounds good and dandy but in reality we know it doesn't work that easy. Just think about it, the youths of today are out of control. Yes, you have your exceptions but overall, these kids now a days make Dennis the Menace look like an angel.

All these challenges are there despite all your experts, doctors, and every book on the subject of rearing children. So, as you can see, it's not easy. If you are a parent, you can relate. And if you are not, and you would like to have children, I suggest you gather as much knowledge and suggestions as possible from those who have been successful in rearing children so you can have a fighting chance when yours come around. Now remember, no two kids are the same, so the knowledge you gain is like a data bank in your brain that you can draw from when certain scenarios or incidents happen with your children that will help you successfully meet that challenge. Sometimes, you will deal with new challenges. Like Forrest Gump's mother said: *"Life is like a box of chocolates."* When this happens, remain calm and use common sense to solve the problem. You do not want to overreact or else they will never come to you for advice or to tell you their problems and concerns. No matter how much you disagree with them or hate what you are hearing, bite your tongue and listen. It is the only way you can find out the truth and be in a better position to help them. Reason with your children. Persuade them to come to a correct decision by using illustrations and questions that reach their hearts and minds. Paint a picture of the outcome or consequences of making a bad decision.

The most important thing is to instill in your children Godly principles and a loving fear of God from when they are young. It is the best advice anyone can give you. A wholesome fear of God is a protection. Children thrive under discipline. They may not tell you this but children need a sense of direction despite their attitude at times. All children want to know and feel that they are loved and that we sincerely care about them especially as their parents. They feed off of this. It's interesting to note that youths who join gangs stay in gangs because they feel like they have a family, and they protect and care for each other as a family, and this draws them to this way of life. So, never stop loving or telling your kids you love them, no matter how frustrating rearing them at times can get. Love never fails. With proper training and spirituality in a child's life, you can succeed in rearing kids. Also keep in mind that old saying: "The fruit does not fall far from the tree." So, consider your children's behavior, keeping in mind the traits and personalities that, perhaps through no fault of their own, they have inherited from someone in the family. Or, just think back to when you were young and don't be surprised if you see a lot of you in him or her. Of course, this is no excuse for bad behavior. However, it does help us to be somewhat understanding and compassionate when training our children. Also, if you know how the person turned out that your child is like, you will have an idea how your child will grow up and you will be in a better position to help him or her. This will also help you to make needed changes and adjustments in your discipline and counsel that you give your children when and if they begin to stray. If the person is doing well, this will give you hope when dealing with your children, especially during those trying times in his or her stage in life.

Granted, you may have a black sheep in the family and nothing you can do will help that person until they hit rock bottom or die young because of the decisions they made, and, yes, it will bring you sadness, anxiety, and stress in your life. You may even regret having children. But, don't blame yourself for the outcome if you have done all you can to love them and nurture them. Those are the chances you take. In this imperfect world, nothing is a guarantee. This being said, I can see why the Bible says children are a gift from God. They bring you a joy and happiness unlike any other. It's a feeling only a parent can relate to. From the moment they are born, your whole life changes. You immediately see the responsibility you now have to love and protect this little life. You will not think twice to get in front of a train, if it meant saving your child's life. Those special moments, such as first word, first step, first smile, and first dance are priceless. I would never trade them in for anything the world has to offer. I am blessed to have two beautiful kids. Has it been challenging at times? Yes, it sure has and many of you would agree as you consider your own families but in the end it's all worth it. In fact, I would agree that children, at least in my case, can make you a better person. As human beings, we learn many things in life. Through adversity, we learn success. Though failure, we learn Godliness. Through endurance, we learn how to love. Through kindness, we learn compassion toward others. Even though at times it's very unpleasant to undergo various trials in child rearing, we all become better people if we successfully meet these challenges and allow them to refine us and make us better individuals. Those same Godly qualities we use in dealing with our children, will in time be used with many with whom we come in contact in our journey through life.

Remember to get involved in every aspect of raising your child. Feeding your baby is a precious time. This is the closet you will get to that maternal feeling woman get. Learn how to change diapers for you will enjoy how your child stares at you and you will enjoy your baby playing with its fingers and feet. Trust me, these are beautiful moments as you bond with your child. Learn how to bathe the baby. I know initially you feel that the mother is better qualified to do this and its true, woman have a maternal instinct which it seems they do this all with ease, but don't be afraid. You will learn and in time you will truly enjoy it. These moments are magical so don't lose out by not getting involved. This nurturing process is vital as you bond with your child. This will truly endear you to your baby. This is fatherhood. Anyone can have a baby. There are idiots having kids all the time. Being a father is a whole different ball game. Now you are fulfilling your God given role in the family circle. Every child needs a father. So, before you decide to have children, make sure you are ready for the responsibility. If you are, then children are truly a gift from God. There will be times during those difficult teenage years that will test your will but whatever you do, never give up. Try to think before you say something hurtful to your child that you will regret later on. Find ways to compromise without setting aside your principles. Be a good listener and do not overreact when they approach you with a problem or a question, for If you do, they will never again go to you. Instead, they will choose another, most likely someone with less experience than you. So take a deep breath, say a prayer, yell into a pillow, or whatever works for you. Just don't over react and drive your child away. Help him or her to see that their best friends are their parents. Like God, you want what's best for them. Give them their space but let them know that it's based on trust. The more trustworthy they are, the more space they will get. Give them privacy yet monitor it by asking questions all the time. Where are you going? Who's going with you? What are you watching or listening to? You get the picture. They may not always like it and that's ok. They will get over it. Be involved, while at the same time, giving them their space and privacy. As long as they live under your roof, you have every right to set rules. All of this is a form of training that will help them when they go out into the real world. And you hope that when they are on their own, they will look back and appreciate all that you have done and call you to tell you how much they appreciate all that you did for them. When they do it, then all will be worth it. Then, the struggles, the challenges, the teenage years, will all seem like a distinct past.

Once they have reached young adulthood, you struggle with the fact that to them it's not cool to hang out with their parents no matter how cool and down to earth you may be. Now, if you are nerdy by nature, I could understand why your kids will not go out with you. Still, you should encourage them to set aside time for their folks, or do as I did, and make them go out with you to the movies, restaurants and other places. Choose a night during a weekend and make plans with them with no exception. In the beginning, they fuss a lot but eventually it gets better and now we enjoy each other's company. It's also cool when you can go out with them when they become 21 and over. I enjoy going out with my daughter. It's a different experience seeing your kids grow up and now you are actually enjoying their company both as your children and also as friends, perhaps dancing together or enjoying a drink together. So, stay close to your children. Avoid arguments or feuds that will put you apart. Learn to compromise on Issues that are not so important or serious in nature. Remember to respect their opinion and listen to their point of view, even if you do not agree. It's terrible when parents and children do not speak to each other because of some disagreement or misunderstanding. If that has happened to you, take care of it. Do not let precious time go by because you never know when it could be your last day or theirs, and you would regret this for the rest of your life. As a parent, remembers you are still the adult to them. Do not let stubbornness or pride get in the way of a wonderful relationship with your kids. Take it from me, you will regret it. I missed my daughter's 21-year-old first drink because I overreacted. If you do, you will miss these special moments in your children's lives and some of those moments only happen once in a while or only once in their lives.

The next stage in their adult lives is when they meet someone. This could be a wonderful time for the whole family, especially if they find someone who truly loves them and takes care of them, and shares your religious convictions. Really, that is all you want as a parent. Now, my rule is simple: never get involved in your children's relationships unless your opinion or suggestion is asked for. The only time you get involved is if your child, especially if you have a daughter, is being abused physically. Then, you follow Sonny Corleone's rule to let him know that she has a daddy and he is the only one who has the God-given right to spank her if she needs discipline. So, you remind him how it feels by following Sonny's rule. You also remind him that she has lots of cousins who also follow this rule. If your daughter decides to forgive him, remind him that in this case there are no second chances. He will regret if you have to come back. Besides this issue, let your children work out their own marriage just like you did. Be good in-laws. Statistics show that many marriages end up in divorce because of the in-laws. The Bible says to let no man put apart what God has yoked together. Great wisdom in these words for all in-laws to follow. Give these young newlyweds a chance to succeed in their marriage. In the end, your hope in life now is to see your children happy, and if they choose to have children to then spoil your grandchildren. This is the normal process in family relationships.

God created the family unit and blessed us with the ability to procreate. Our children are gifts from God but in reality they belong to Him, so rear them to be God-fearing people. Inculcate in them Bible principles that will help them for a life time. If they stray to the left or right, don't overreact. Be loving and in a kind way give your children needed direction and instructions to help them get back on track. It may take them a while. Just remember when you were young and be patient. Never give up on your kids. The example you give them will be invaluable to them and will mold their lives for the future.

Fulfill your role in the family circle and you will have a successful family unit. Love and enjoy your children for they are a wonderful gift from God.

CHAPTER 8
The In-Laws

I will be remised to write a book and not write about the in-laws, especially since it would seem that the wife is the one who gets the brunt of the problems. They made a sitcom over the issue of mother-in-laws and daughter-in-laws. The sitcom, *"Everyone Loves Raymond,"* in a funny way, illustrates the conflict between the two. If you watch the show, you will see how true many of their humorous skids are about the constant battle between the ladies. I saw it for myself in my marriage with my mother in the beginning of our marriage and no doubt you can relate to it in one form or another in your relationship.

Now granted, some of it may seem exaggerated and that's to make the show funny but a lot of it is true and we laugh because many of our mates can relate to the skits. Raymond was a trip and we can see a little of ourselves in Raymond especially if we are close to our moms and we find ourselves in the middle of two women we love. It's not easy. I do agree that there are many moms like Raymond's mom out there driving our beautiful wives crazy. Now seeing it for myself and experiencing it firsthand, I offer no excuse for their behavior. But perhaps, if we understand why some behave this way, it can help us cope and make the best of it just like Raymond's wife Diane does in the show. Believe it or not, we can also show a measure of compassion. Before you scream, let me explain why I say this.

Diane shows us that even though she blows up at times in the end they all make up and it all starts all over again. She is never going to change her mother-in-law and that may be your situation but her constant love for her husband may, eventually to some degree, win over her mother-in-law so they can at least coexist. This eventually was my experience. Now my wife and mother get along great. It wasn't easy and it took years. But take it from me, there is hope.

So let me explain my theory as to why I believe mothers-in-law, especially when it comes to men, behave this way and for this reason, may in a little small amount, deserve a measure of compassion. Yes, compassion.

When I got married and I had the mother and son first dance, my mother told me something that I think explains why mothers in the beginning are at times very hard on our wives. Even though this is my theory, it makes sense.

My mother told me: "When I was raising you, I dreamed of the time when you would grow up and get a job and spend time with me by taking me out to dinner, the movies, and other places. Then, just when I thought this was going to happen, you got married and now you are going to forget all about me and do everything with her." You would have to agree that this was such a real moment for me and is the reason why our moms may at times — not all the time — deserve a compassionate heart. Of course, I looked at her and told her that will never happen. But the reality is, this is how they feel and would explain their behavior, or at least make some kind of sense to this insanity between the in-laws.

You have to remember you are their little boy who they have been taking care of you all your life — feeding you, bathing you, and dressing you, and as you get older, giving you advice and instructions through out your teenage years. The motherly bond is as great as ever and now here come this other woman into your life and all your time and energy is redirected to this other person. Of course, you love your mother but your time is limited now and so your mother is the odd one out. So, you see ladies, like I said, it doesn't excuse their behavior but you could understand why perhaps they get so involved in your relationship. It's years of nurturing a boy to adulthood and then just because he falls in love, her relationship with her son is over or ends right away. As imperfect humans, it is possible it's going to be a struggle but, if you don't drive each other crazy, it does get better or at least bearable. As they see you loving and taking care of their baby boy, they feel more assured and comfortable that he is happy and they tend not to be as involved until you have kids and then that's another story.

Now, this is my advice to you husbands. Keep in mind that the struggle of in-laws are real and in many cases they become a factor and cause for many divorces in the world. They make movies and shows concerning the in-law dilemma. They make us laugh when we are watching them but the sad fact is that they make our wives' life miserable when we let it get out of control in the real world. We hold the key to a wonderful relationship between the in-laws. Remember, we can do no wrong in our mothers' eyes but our wives, well that's another story.

So, if you want your marriage to last forever, heed the proverbial saying in the Bible: let no man put apart what God has yoked together. Stick to your mate no matter what. Give her the benefit of the doubt and never say my mother would never say or do that. Trust me, when I tell you that when you hear the horror stories of in-laws and there are many, listen to your wife and support her. Also, you should never take sides with your parents against your mate, even if she is in the wrong. If she is wrong, help her to see why she is wrong and discuss it as a couple and don't get the in-laws involved or tell them what she said because that is between you and your wife. As her husband, what is said in your home and between each other is private. A real man respects his wife and doesn't try to embarrass her or reveal her confidential talk with her husband.

Now, the in-laws will try to get involved by either complaining or attacking your mate. It will be a constant battle between you and your mother. She will try to sway your thinking by constantly bringing up incidents pass or present to show your mate's faults or imperfections. They will try to involve others by saying that they too feel the same way about your mate. This is done by gossiping about the problem that may exist between your mate and mother-in-law. Whatever you do, never except or allow your mother to talk bad about the person you love. I believe a real man would never allow this to happen. Let her know that you will not entertain her comments and if she continues to speak negative or accuse her of things she said or did that you know are not true, you will stop answering the phone until she stops talking about your mate. Don't let yourself get into this cycle. I have been there and it does not stop until you make it clear that you support your spouse 100 percent and that it has nothing to do about how you feel about your mother. She knows you love her. However, you let your mother know that she is your wife and mother of your children and you will not allow anyone, including your mother, talk bad about her.

Once they see how serious and committed you are to your mate, they normally start excepting her into the family. I guess they figure if you can't beat them might as well join them. And in time, things will get better. Like any relationship, it's just a matter of understanding and respecting each other and learning to give and take so that in the end peace and love prevail. You thus avoid becoming a statistic in the percentage of marriages ending because of the in-laws.

Your spouse will respect you for supporting her and your giving her unconditional love. God's wisdom is far superior to ours and He says the two will become one flesh so let no man put apart what God has yoked together. If we listen to this wise saying, we will succeed as a couple with any issues, including the in-laws.

As a word of advice, do not go to mom when you have problems at home as this would only add to the tensions that exist or may develop between the in-laws. No matter how tempting it is to talk to mom, who you know will always side with you, you need someone who will not be bias and will give you advice whether you like it or not. Plus, mom doesn't need to know your business. A man takes care of his own household and respects his mate by not talking to others about his problems with his wife. He realizes that this will only make matters worse and, in fact, encourages mom to get involved in your marriage. This in not a good recipe for success.

Ladies, I'm sure you are wondering how long this battle will last between the in-laws. Well, I'm sorry to tell you, there is not a set time. If you are fortunate, hopefully not long at all or it could take years. In some cases, it may never end and you just learn to deal or cope with it. It doesn't hurt to put on a show, or pretend you get along, for the sake of the children or family. The good news is that on average the disagreements and fighting stops when the in-laws see that you, the husband, is committed and supportive of your mate. Mom especially, when she realizes that her efforts are producing no results in her favor, may change her position. If you have a neutral dad, this will help because mom will normally complain to him after she is done with you. Since he is a man, he respects the fact that no one should interfere in someone else's marriage unless it's his daughter's and she is being abused mentally and physically, then all bets are off. However, for the most part, dad will always have your back. This is a good thing for the constant battle between the in-laws can get very tiresome and frustrating, since it involves people you love.

Now, my advice to you ladies is simple — the less you say to your mother-in-law when issues arise the better. You are not going to win so pick your battles. If your problem continues, let your husband do all the talking with his mother. The reason that's important is because you will be accused of saying something unkind or disrespectful, which in most cases never happened, so do yourself a favor and avoid interacting with your mother-in-law until she gets better. Also, try very hard not to talk about your in-laws. Remember, they are parents to your spouse and no one likes to hear criticism about their folks all the time even though they are in the wrong. Let your husband take care of it. Be patient and understanding. Perhaps, you can win them over without saying a word by your actions and remember love conquers all and time heals most wounds. Do not let this chapter in your life affect your marriage. Keep in mind, this is not unique to you only, as most couples go through an episode in one form or another with their in-laws. Like all experiences in life, it will make you a better person because someday you may be an in-law to your kids.

The in-laws can truly be a blessing in a family. Granted, it can be tough at times but for the most part they are a great help, especially if you have children. They also have a wealth of experience and advice we can draw from and it's nice to have family dinners together from time to time.

You know what? Let's just all try to get along together, respect one another, give each other space to grow, and try to meddle only in matters that pertain to your family. Word of advice to all you in-laws: if your kids are happy and are being treated right, don't change that. Don't be the cause of your children's marital problems or failures. How sad it would be to look back at the happenings of your children only to see them depressed and by themselves because your actions caused their divorce. You will never forgive yourself and you may possibly lose a son's love. Instead, be happy for your children and do your part to help him or her have a successful and happy marriage. In the end, isn't this what you want for your children? Isn't this what you wanted when you were married? Watch *"Monster In Law,"* the great movie that can help us all appreciate this point.

CHAPTER 9
What Have We Learned?

There is no doubt based on observation and experience, and life as a whole, that women are amazing creatures who should be loved, respected, and cherished.

Sadly though, throughout history, we have seen woman mistreated, abused, exploited, and treated like second-class citizens. This awful behavior still exist in some parts of the world where there are places that woman are killed just for looking at another man. How barbaric is that! And, of course, you have those who abuse woman physically and mentally and still claim they love them. These idiots have no clue what love is. Why would you want to hurt or bruise someone you love? Why don't you try beating yourself first against a wall or slapping yourself around, before you touch anyone else? A man who treats a woman in such a way is a coward who needs help.

Always remember how beautiful she was when you first met her and decided to marry her because of her inner or outer beauty and that's how she should remain under your care. It is your loving responsibility to protect her at all cost even with your life if need be for she is your better half. No matter how bad things may get, abuse should never be an option. Learn to deal with your problems through understanding and respect. There is no place for this cowardly behavior in any relationship, especially in a loving household.

Instead, she should be the queen of her home. Let her take care of the affairs of the house and sit back and see how great she is. Now, I'm not advocating doing nothing or being a couch potato. Now a days, it takes two to take care of a home, especially if both are working secularly. What I mean is that women like their home a certain way. They like things done a certain way. Yea, it may seem to us men like nothing but it means a lot to them and that's what's important. There is nothing like a happy woman in her own household. I'm sure you have witnessed a moody crabby person so take your pick. It's a no brainer, if you know what I mean. All kidding aside, we should try our best to make those whom we love happy. There is no better way.

Besides considering all they do, it is the least we can do for these incredible people in our lives. For my part, I am truly lost without my wife. She means that much to me. My only regret is that I did not take care of her as well as I should of and perhaps all you men out there can relate to this. But, it's never too late if you are still with the one you love to continue to make progress in your relationship. Reflect on your life and see if you need to make changes to make things better.

As imperfect humans, we have the tendency to take for granted those we love, especially our dear wives. So, it's important that from time to time all of us men should take a look at our relationship to make sure that it's still on a course to happiness or if it needs a little or big tweak. Like everything in life, whether it's a car, house, or our bodies, it needs to be maintained, and if not, it will stop working eventually. Wear and tear takes a toll on everything. Well, our relationships are no different. They need maintaining to continue to be successful for we live in a world full of stress and anxieties and challenges that take a toll on a marriage. At times, those challenges become overwhelming in a relationship and begin to breakdown a happy relationship, so it's vital for us to honestly talk to our mates and listen to them to see what needs to be adjusted and maintained and what needs to be done to remain happy. Now, a word of caution to you ladies — take baby steps if changes are needed.

Men normally don't make rapid progress. Remember, we are like this since youth. Little girls always do things earlier than little boys; they even grow faster. However, in time, we do make needed changes, especially when we feel we are losing the one we love. Also, don't expect perfection. Sometimes, it feels that nothing we do is good enough and whether it's so or not, it's how many of us men feel. So be realistic and reasonable with the changes that need to be made and balanced as to your expectations. Love is patient and kind. Love never fails. Do your best to do your part in helping your mate make progress.

Now, you men cherish the one you love. Take care of the store figuratively speaking or someone else will take care of it for you. Make no room for the devil. He doesn't need our help to destroy families and marriages.

Love and appreciate these beautiful people in society. They are the backbone and, in most cases, the brains in all relationships. Listen to them and you will succeed in life. I learned this growing up with mom and I have confirmed this with my wife … for women are amazing.

Brief Biography of Author

Armando Guerra has always been intrigued by human relationships and the inspiration of his wife's unconditional love for 36 years. He began writing his thoughts after keenly observing life as it unfolds. He truly believes that all women should be cherished and loved. His hope is that the book can perhaps help many more see how beautiful and unique these individuals are.

His wife Jacqueline affectionately called Jackie is a finance major. She has always been financially sound and organized. Her independent spirit allows her to keep their family very balanced and happy. They both like to travel and together they have been able to enjoy many beautiful destinations around the world and this has allowed them to bond together as a couple. Armando and Jackie share a passionate love for life and each other.

Armando's life is also surrounded by the love of his children Vanessa and Ryan. According to Armando, both of their children inherited their mother's DNA for smarts and looks. He has two beautiful grandchildren Everli and Emelia and has a great son in law Bryant. Together they make up a family who love each other dearly but more important their faith in God helps them to understand the role all of them play in making their family life successful and strong.

Faith in God and strong family bonds are the fabric of Armando's life. Without this balance he feels one just lives in a house.

www.ingramcontent.com/pod-product-compliance
Lightning Source LLC
Chambersburg PA
CBHW030112070426
42448CB00036B/761